Simple Maths

Doubling and Multiplying

Richard Leff

Raintree

www.raintreepublishers.co.uk

Visit our website to find out more information about **Raintree** books.

To order:

 Phone 44 (0) 1865 888112

Send a fax to 44 (0) 1865 314091

Visit the Raintree Bookshop at **www.raintreepublishers.co.uk** to browse our catalogue and order online.

First published in Great Britain by Raintree, Halley Court, Jordan Hill, Oxford OX2 8EJ, part of Harcourt Education.
Raintree is a registered trademark of Harcourt Education Ltd.

Editorial: Diyan Leake and Cassie Mayer
Design: Joanna Hinton-Malivoire and
  The Partnership
Picture Research: Erica Newbery
Production: Duncan Gilbert

Originated by Modern Age
Printed and bound in China by
  South China Printing Company

10 digit ISBN 1 4062 0392 0 (hardback)
13 digit ISBN 978 1 4062 0392 9
10 09 08 07 06
10 9 8 7 6 5 4 3 2 1

10 digit ISBN 1 4062 0397 1 (paperback)
13 digit ISBN 978 1 4062 0397 4
11 10 09 08 07
10 9 8 7 6 5 4 3 2 1

British Library Cataloguing in Publication Data
Leffingwell, Richard
Doubling and Multiplying
513.2'13
A full catalogue record for this book is available from the British Library.

Acknowledgements
The publishers would like to thank the following for permission to reproduce photographs: Getty Images (Photodisc Red/Davies & Starr) p. **22**; Harcourt Education Ltd (www.mmstudios.co.uk) pp. **4–18**, **20**, back cover

Cover photograph reproduced with permission of Getty Images (DK Images/Andy Crawford).

The publishers would like to thank Patti Barber, Specialist in Early Childhood and Primary Education, Institute of Education, University of London, for his/her assistance in the preparation of this book.

Every effort has been made to contact copyright holders of any material reproduced in this book. Any omissions will be rectified in subsequent printings if notice is given to the publishers.

The paper used to print this book comes from sustainable resources.

Contents

What is doubling?

What does it look like when you see double?

You see two of everything.

Doubling flowers

2 + 2

When you double 2, you add 2
and 2 together.

2 x 4

Adding the same numbers together is a way of multiplying.

You put together two groups that are both the same.

Doubling marbles

Look what happens when you keep doubling a number.

Start by doubling 1.

$$2 \times 1 = 2$$

Now double 2.

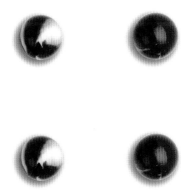

$$2 \times 2 = 4$$

Now double 4.

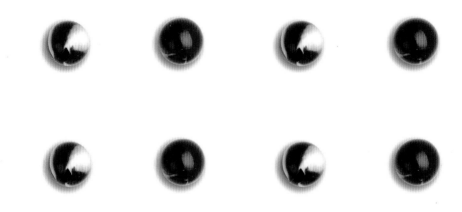

$$2 \times 4 = 8$$

Learning doubles will help you learn multiplication.

Can you double 8?

2 x 8 = ?

Doubling stars

What happens when you double 3?

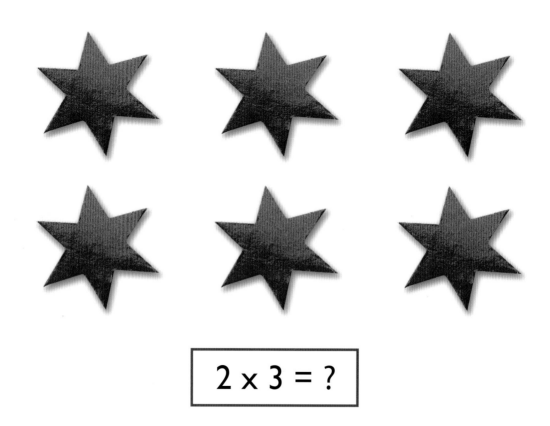

$$2 \times 3 = ?$$

When you double 3, you add 2 groups of 3 together.

Now try doubling 6.

2 x 6 = ?

Can you double 12?

2 x 12 = ?

You can keep on doubling as long as you like.

Can you double 24?

It might be hard.

2 x 24 = ?

Doubling buttons

What if you double 5?

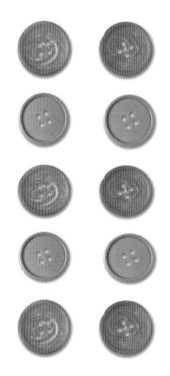

2 x 5 = ?

What if you double 10?

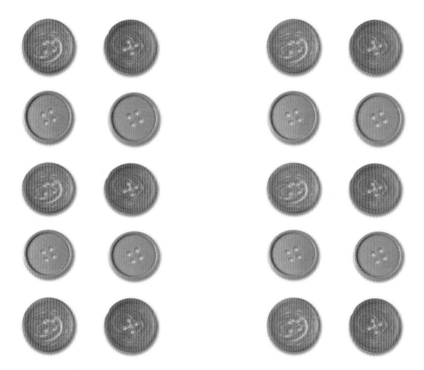

$$2 \times 10 = ?$$

Practising doubling

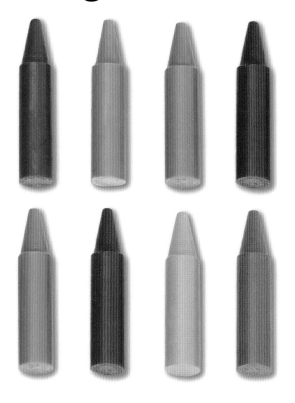

$$2 \times 4 = ?$$

It seems like when you double something you end up with more.

Is this always true?

What would happen if you doubled nothing?

$$2 \times 0 = 0$$

You still have nothing!

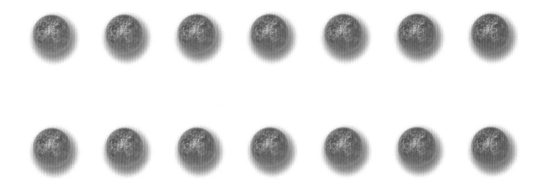

$$2 \times 7 = 14$$

When you double something you are adding the same number.

You are multiplying by 2.

$$2 \times 4 = 8$$

$$2 \times 5 = 10$$

$$2 \times 6 = 12$$

$$2 \times 7 = 14$$

$$2 \times 8 = 16$$

Doubling can be fun.

How old would you be if you doubled your age?

Quiz

Can you answer this doubling question?

$$2 \times 7 = ?$$

Hint: You need to add 2 groups of 7 together.

The "times" sign

| x | You use this sign to show that you are multiplying numbers. |

$$2 \times 3$$

When you multiply 2 by 3, you get 6.

| = | You use the equals sign to show what 2 times 3 is equal to. |

$$2 \times 3 = 6$$

Index

Answer to the quiz on page 22

$2 \times 7 = 14$

Note to parents and teachers

Reading non-fiction texts for information is an important part of a child's literacy development. Readers can be encouraged to ask simple questions and then use the text to find the answers. Most chapters in this book begin with a question. Read the questions together. Look at the pictures. Talk about what the answer might be. Then read the text to find out if your predictions were correct. To develop readers' enquiry skills, encourage them to think of other questions they might ask about the topic. Discuss where you could find the answers. Assist children in using the contents page, picture glossary and index to practise research skills and new vocabulary.